Toys of the Past Fifty Years

Brian Moses

Barry, Diana, Kerry, Josh

Barry

Hello, I'm Barry and this is my
family. I was born in 1954 in England.

Barry as a boy

Toys from
the 1950s

When I was a boy in the
1950s, I played with toy cars
made of metal.
Later on, I had a clockwork
train. I had to wind it up with a key to make it
go. Have you ever seen a clockwork train?

Diana

Diana as a girl

Some dolls from the 1960s

Sindy

POP SINGER

Pedigree

This is my wife, Diana. When she was a little girl, she had lots of dolls. She liked to dress them. Did you know the first Barbie doll was made in 1959?

Later on, Diana had a hula hoop. She had to wiggle her hips to make the hula hoop spin.

Fun with a hula hoop

3

Then, in the 1970s, schools had LEGO® bricks. Boys and girls built houses, boats and cars. They liked playing with LEGO® bricks. Do you have LEGO® bricks in your classroom?

At school in the 1970s

Some LEGO® models

Boys and girls often took their own toys to school. Boys had Action Man dolls dressed in army clothes. At that time, it was a new thing to see boys playing with dolls.

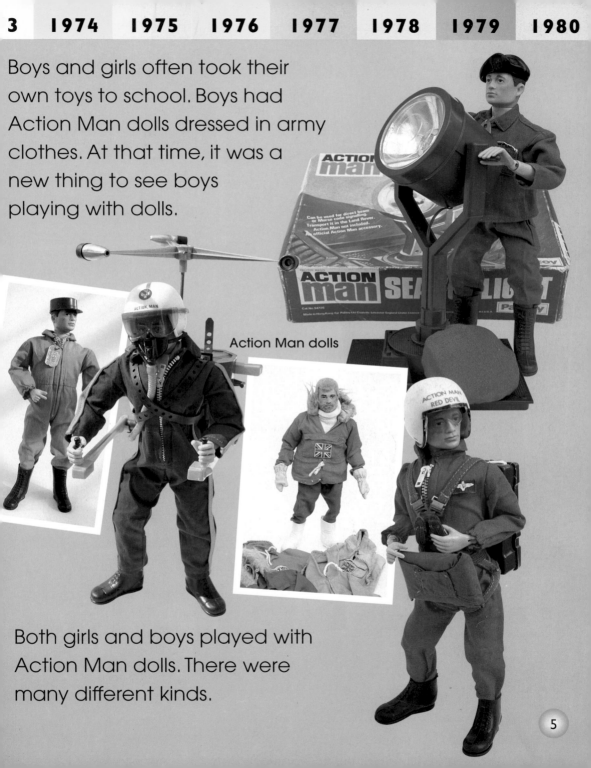

Action Man dolls

Both girls and boys played with Action Man dolls. There were many different kinds.

5

Kerry as a young girl

Our daughter Kerry was born in 1987.

First of all, she liked to play with Barbie dolls.

Kerry with her dolls

Next she played with My Little Pony toys. When she was older, she liked to play on her skateboard.

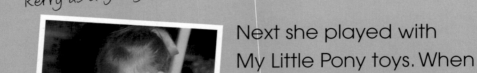

My Little Pony

A skateboard

6

Our son Josh was born
in 1995.
When he was older, he liked
to play with LEGO® bricks.
Later on, he liked to play on
his Game Boy. His favourite
game was Pokémon.

Josh as a baby

Josh as a young boy

A LEGO®
racing car

A PlayStation

After that, he had a
PlayStation and a LEGO®
racing car for his birthday.

Do you have a
favourite game?

Toys today are very different from the ones that I had fifty years ago.

I don't know what sort of toys children will play with in the next fifty years.

One thing I do know is that children will still be having fun with them.